Hawai'i

Vortex Field Guide

Island Vortex Series #1

By Zach Royer

Other books by Zach Royer:

"Pyramid Rising: Planetary Acupuncture to Combat Climate Change" (Read a preview in the back of this book)

"Kona Haunted Hele Guidebook"

Follow my research into supernatural Hawai'i!

www.KahunaResearchGroup.org
www.BigIslandParanormal.com
www.BigIslandParanormal.net
www.BigIslandParanormal.org

Search Google for
"The 52 Supernatural Places on Hawai'i Island"

Hawai'i Vortex Field Guide – Island Vortex Series #1
Copyright © 2014 *Zach Royer, Kahuna Research Group*
All rights reserved.
Keeping it local…Written and published in Hawai'i
Printed in the U.S.A.
ISBN: 978-1495308369
Original cover art by Zach Royer © 2014
10 9 8 7 6 5 4 3 2 1
Black & White Edition

Made in the USA
Charleston, SC
24 March 2015

This page is good for one regular $7 admission at Paleaku Gardens Peace Sanctuary. Please present this page at time of visit. Mahalo.

Big Island of Hawai'i

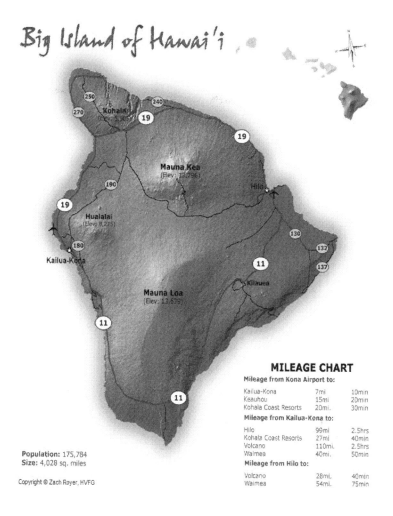

Population: 175,784
Size: 4,028 sq. miles

Copyright © Zach Royer, HVFG

MILEAGE CHART

Mileage from Kona Airport to:

Kailua-Kona	7mi	10min
Keauhou	15mi	20min
Kohala Coast Resorts	20mi.	30min

Mileage from Kailua-Kona to:

Hilo	99mi	2.5hrs
Kohala Coast Resorts	27mi	40min
Volcano	110mi.	2.5hrs
Waimea	40mi.	50min

Mileage from Hilo to:

Volcano	28mi.	40min
Waimea	54mi.	75min

Thank You

My connection with the land has deepened tremendously after writing about and experiencing the vortexes necessary for this guide book. My deepest thanks go to the Earth and to Hawai'i for being such a beautiful, wondrous place to live. I'm in love with nature, and it feels like nature is in love with me.

Thank you (yes, you) for buying or borrowing a copy of this book, your support is much appreciated. Thanks also to my closest friends & family for being on this adventure called life with me. I am especially grateful to the late Bruce Cathie and Ivan T. Sanderson, who both continue inspiring me to explore from beyond the veil. Your research has proven invaluable for many of us over the years.

Finally, thank you to all that have lovingly and generously shared their experiences with me. Your stories have inspired me and for that I am truly blessed.

Z. Royer - Hawai'i Island - November 2014

Table of Contents

Author's Preface

Destination Paradise..13

How Sites Become Sacred......................................17

Hawaii's Healing Energy..23

Earth's Subtle Energy Field.....................................31

Identifying Vortexes..43

- ⊕ Mauna Kea Vortex..59
- ⊕ Mauna Loa Vortex...63
- ⊕ Kilauea Vortex...71
- ⊕ Kalani Vortex...79
- ⊕ Punaluu Vortex..83
- ⊕ South Point Vortex..87
- ⊕ Place of Refuge Vortex..................................93
- ⊕ Paleaku Vortex..97
- ⊕ Kealakekua Vortex..101
- ⊕ Waimea Vortex..105
- ⊕ Waipio Valley Vortex.....................................109
- ⊕ Hamakulia Vortex..113

Other Famous Vortexes..129

A New Beginning..132

Returning Home...134

Author's Profile..137

References & Websites..139

Mileage Chart...151

Author's Preface

Aloha! Thank you for your interest and support of the *Hawai'i Vortex Field Guide*, which was inspired by the dozens of sacred sites here on the Big Island and others around the world.

Get ready for your journey through paradise as I lead you to the far corners of the island, visiting locations that are both beautiful and mystifying. The *Hawai'i Vortex Field Guide* is your guide to a dozen sacred vortexes that are found around the Big Island. As you visit the sacred sites detailed in this field guide, allow yourself a chance to absorb the energies and enjoy the visual spectacles that you will find there and along the way.

At the beginning of each of the twelve vortexes in this book, I detail the **Type**, **Strength**, **Accessibility**, **Attractions**, and **Directions** to each location as best as I could. I also give a detailed description of each vortex based on personal experiences, a quick fact and then why the area is considered sacred. There are even a few sections for

you to keep notes of your adventure; I hope you get to use them.

Assuming you are staying in either Kona or Hilo, that's where I give starting directions from in this guide. Navigating the Big Island is not all that hard...there is just one major highway, Highway 11, and it goes both North and South around the entire island, connecting in one big loop. Some of the locations mentioned in this book are just off the main roadway, while others may require a small hike to get to, while some are offshore and can't be reached too easily.

I recommend you get plenty of rest the night before you set out, drink plenty of water, and take plenty of time. It may take two days or more for you to fully assimilate the new experiences that lie ahead...they call it the *Big Island* for a reason!

In between your adventuring, the local farmers markets in Kona or Hilo offer unique fruits & treasures that show signs of a culture steeped in mystery and lore. Each of these places offers exclusive nourishment for your body and soul. Eating

the local foods is an excellent way to connect with the energies of the land (aina).

Keep in mind that Hawai'i can have very rough waters on occasion depending on the surf as well as steep hiking trails and sharp rocks so always be extra careful. Please. I can't stress that enough. Hundreds of visitors are rescued each year while hiking or swimming, while dozens more are less fortunate. Some areas are extremely remote and take hours to access. It is my hope that if you do set out to explore some of the sites around the island or mentioned in this book, you keep to the marked trails, always practice safety when swimming, and please don't disturb any of the historical structures you may come across.

It's also suggested that you don't take any lava rocks off the island as Hawaiians consider them sacred, and the fact that dozens are returned each year because they've caused bad luck to those that take them.

Grab your hat, put on some sunscreen, and make sure your tanks are full. It's time to begin our tropical vortex adventure!

Destination: Paradise

Take a deep breath. Step into a new relationship not only with the Earth – but with your life, and your time in Hawai'i. From the snow-capped Mauna Kea & Mauna Loa Mountains to the lush jungles around Hilo or the sun-drenched beaches of Kona, the island of Hawai'i provides a never-ending panorama of the elements interacting with one another, and with you.

Each day, we should spend time in contemplation of the way the Earth works with the elements of fire, earth, wind and water to create the physical reality in which we come to know ourselves. Through these adventures we learn how to create and manifest memories (and possibly more) in the way the Earth manifests flowers and animals.

On these sacred islands, as well as many other places around the world, one finds evidence of sacred sites that are often times associated with religion and mythology. These sites tend to be marked in one form or another, most typically with

stone, because stone was easily accessible during the time when the site was declared.

Here in Hawai'i, sacred sites are typically marked by what's called a *heiau* (pronounced *hay – yow*), or an *Ahu*, which are both ancient stone structures resembling a cross between the Scottish "cairn" and the Central or South American step pyramid. These represent a special place in the landscape where one can "capture a current of earth energy." Sacred places in Hawai'i are often related to death, war and other aspects of the state's history. If you see lava rocks forming a circle around an area please don't disturb them and don't step over the rocks (you could be disturbing a visiting spirit). The penalty for disturbing these sites is $10,000.

Visiting the most remote islands in the world is a must for anyone seeking the journey of a lifetime, however living here is an adventure all by itself. Active volcanoes, complete with captivating lava flows, wild & friendly dolphins and the occasional *honu*, the sea turtle, along with some of the best fruits nature has to offer are here year round just waiting to enjoy.

The name "Hawai'i" comes from the Polynesian word *Havaiki*, which means "homeland" or "paradise". Hawai'i has been the homeland of the Native Hawaiian people for more than 2,000 years, and it is recognized as a paradise by many others because of its incredible beauty. Hawai'i's official nickname is the Aloha State. "Aloha" is a Hawaiian word that means "love" and "affection". It is used as a greeting and a farewell. The Hawaiians consider treating one another with "aloha" to be the highest form of civilized behavior.

Believed to be the first Hawaiian Island discovered and settled by Polynesians, perhaps as early as the fifth century, Hawai'i's Big Island has been the scene of many of the state's historic events.

The birthplace of King Kamehameha I, this land was the one from which he launched forays to unify the islands. For a time, it was the capital of the kingdom. Hawai'i's Big Island was also the scene of King Kamehameha I's death, and with it the end of the Kapu (laws to protect Hawaiian spirituality) system, abolished by his successor (and son) Kamehameha II in 1819. Kealakekua Bay, Captain James Cook's first Big Island landfall in 1779, and the scene of his death, is the site where the first Christian service (a seaman's burial) was performed on Hawai'i's shores.

Today, much of Hawaii's cultural heritage can still be seen throughout the island, where historical sites have been preserved and made available to the general public. There's always something to do no matter which part of the island you're on. If you're looking for something fun to do in Kona, I take pleasure in leading historical tours along Ali'i Drive with Big Island Ghost Tours to help keep the history, and mystery, alive. There's also a free ticket in the back for Paleaku Gardens Peace Sanctuary in south Kona, one of the sites mentioned in this field guide.

How Sites Become Sacred

When it comes to "sacred geography", a term used to describe a location where the physical environment and spirit meet, Hawai'i is often overlooked among the more famous locations such as Mt. Shasta, Macchu Picchu, Stonehenge or the Great Pyramid, despite being home to the largest & tallest mountains on Earth (Mauna Kea measured from the sea floor and Mauna Loa by mass).

It is believed that the earliest form of sacred geography was to identify natural landscape features as holy, among these were certain mountains, peaks, summits, and cliffs – especially where they formed a landmark, for instance Mauna Kea on the Big Island.

Not just in Hawai'i, but all across the globe, certain areas of subtle energies have been identified by modern researchers, and apparently even ancient man. Many sites have been found to have structures relating to astronomy and religion. Our ancestors were very much in tune with these energies, building structures across various sites around the world.

Before there was a belief in man, there was a belief in Nature. These special places are known as *places of power, sacred sites, power points, power spots,* and *vortexes*. Some would say a place of power is any location with a higher energy concentration than its surroundings.

Image: A stone cairn or 'ahu' atop Mauna Kea. © SacredSites.com

The ancient Hawaiians knew of these mysterious earth energies well, erecting rock temples on the spots where energy was most noticeable. Some of these temples were gigantic, on par with other stone structures around the world. In ancient

Hawai'i, "geomancy", an archaic method of divination based on soil patterns, was practiced and its practitioners were known as *kuhikuhipu'uone*, which means "to point out the sand dunes." They would attune themselves to the subtle energies, similar to a modern day dowser, where they practiced finding hidden objects in the sand. Hawaiian geomancers included psychics, magicians, as well as architects who planned and organized the building of temples, homes, fish ponds, often locating fresh water sources too. They were very tuned in with their surroundings, from the food they grew, to the land they lived on. Hawaiians considered all things sacred, much like Native Americans and many other Native Peoples.

Some theories would even go as far as to suggest that the many stone building, sun worshipping ancient civilizations scattered across the globe were in fact in contact with each other, during a lost and forgotten age of world exploration and that they shared a common knowledge of pre-historic architectural design, evidenced in the many megalithic constructions present throughout the greater Pacific, including those in Pohnpei and Palau.

Not only is the energy wonderful and invigorating at these sites, ancient structures tend to appear, ranging from *heiaus* here in Hawai'i, to step pyramids and stone circles in other countries dating back hundreds to sometimes thousands of years.

In ancient times, with the lack of modern machinery, building a Hawaiian stone *heiau* was no easy task. The architectural feat was typically reserved for only the most celebrated occasions. Flat-topped & smooth-sided despite being constructed with small to medium sized lava rocks (which are irregular and sharp), these structures were often times built by a chief who was encouraged by the advice of his priest, a *kahuna*, who was known to be extremely in tune with nature and the energies of the changing landscape, someone who was even able to control the weather!

Astronomical observations also played a role in determining alignments and constructions of sacred sites. Today, heiau are no longer constructed and unfortunately many of them are subject to destruction as a result of new development. It's only a matter of time before the need to have another

tourist attraction outweighs the need to preserve the history that was once the central focus of an all but forgotten culture.

A deeper exploration into the history of Hawaiian religious architecture might shed some light on why building stone structures here, and elsewhere, is said to bring one closer to Nature, to Spirit, and essentially to God, as is apparent with so many stone building cultures and their religious rituals.

Hawaii's Healing Energy

Hawaii is one of the most powerful and active vortexes on earth, and some vortexes have been known to assist with healing. Each island has a special energy and flavor and many believe the Hawaiian Islands are the *heart chakra system of the plane*t, all of the seven main islands representing and vibrating at a different energy, like the body's unique chakra system.

Hawaii Island Chain / Chakra Parallel

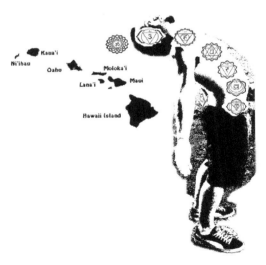

Hawaii is a place of deep healing and divine transformation. Most people who have experienced the magic in Hawaii end up moving here where they are being called as if from a past life. Some also correlate their recurring dreams and early childhood memories back to an ancient and spiritual culture known as *Mu* or sometimes *Lemuruia*. Many travelers come to the islands for more than just a vacation on a beautiful island; they come to heal.

Vortexes are areas of high energy, originating from magnetic, spiritual, or sometimes unknown sources. Additionally they are thought to be gateways or portals to other realms, both spiritual and dimensional. These powerful eddies of pure earth power manifest as spiral-like concentrations of energy that are either electric, magnetic, or electromagnetic qualities of life force.

Besides "earth" vortexes, there are also "body" vortexes, or what others have called Chakras. Chakras are subtle force centers said to channel energy into the body. In Sanskrit the word chakra means "wheel" and they are often seen or shown as

spinning vortexes similar to a spinning wheel or a water drain.

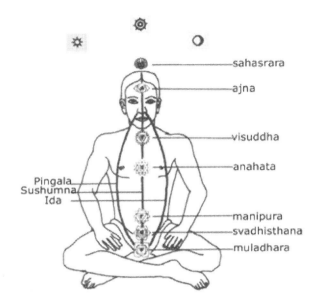

Chakras act as gateways between the higher planes of existence and the physical plane that we perceive. From these 'gates' energy is distributed throughout the body in a system of pathways called Nadis in Sanskrit. The chakras fall, or are created, like Ley Lines, at the points where these lines cross and meet. The differentiation between a major and minor chakra is made by how many and how major these Nadis that cross and meet are. Obviously, the more that meet, and the bigger they are, the more

major the chakra is. The seven major body Vortexes are listed on the previous page.

Each site carries unique energy that exponentially magnifies and quickens whatever intention a person brings to each site. The manifestation vortex is one of the easiest places in the world to instantly manifest anything! Healing sites offers potent concentrations of balancing energy through which miracles can happen. The same is true for other sites, as they all accelerate and amplify intentions in their own unique way. Some of the specific sites on Hawaii Island hold the energy of:

- **Creativity**
- **Death, change and transformation**
- **Pure unconditional love**
- **Healing, Forgiveness and Peace**
- **Birthing**
- **Perfect male/female balance (relationship)**
- **Instant manifestation**
- **Empowerment**

For many people, including me, the ocean "calls" to them and helps them with the healing process. The water off the Kona Coast is circulated from international seas, and there is minimal river run-off so the ocean offers pure salt water for relaxation and healing. The best nature has to offer. When you come to heal, come with respect and humility and openness to the sacred healing centers of the island; for they can sense your intentions.

There is said to be a healing lake that many Hawaiian kahuna and other shamans visit near the top of Mauna Kea that offers mystical experiences. Mauna Kea is considered an ancient vortex that is being triggered open for these times, and it is number one on our list.

If you're looking for a place to heal your life, or are searching for the reasons why you are here in these times, you might want to research Mu or Hawaii and come for a visit. I'd be happy to help you connect with the island or these sites on a personal vortex excursion. The spirit world is more alive and palpable in Hawai'i than almost anywhere in the world. Many have awareness that the islands feel

alive and have a consciousness that assists them as a guide and a mentor. Whether you are a master or beginner on your spiritual path, the islands will meet you exactly where you are with the perfect teaching, quickening and/or transformational process. Everything is amplified and accelerated in Hawaii and there's a sense of timelessness like no other place on earth.

In addition to energetic and metaphysical attributes of the Islands are special physical qualities that stand out. This is perhaps a reason for the unique and transformative power. Each Island evolved by a volcano, or volcanoes that began with a single hot area. There is a high concentration of obsidian, iron and other elements which amplify transformation. Many vortexes have been shown to be associated with the World Grid and have been found to be extremely strong at nodal points where the grid lines cross. Worldwide, the Great Pyramid in Egypt and Stonehenge in England are perhaps the most well known sites of vortex activity.

Because Hawai'i as a whole is known to be a spiritual power spot, a vortex here is a place where one can feel Hawaii's spiritual energy, or *mana*, most strongly. The volcanic mass that makes up the Big Island could be considered one enormous and powerful vortex with all the active volcanism and magnetism that occurs.

Earth's Subtle Energy Field

Hawaiians refer poetically to the volcano goddess *Pele* as continually giving birth to new land, and at a rate of roughly one square mile of new coastline per year, that statement is definitely true. Tremendous varieties of lava in the volcanic landscape combined with the general magnetism of Earth as a whole, means that your body's electric field (aura) is exposed to an ever changing and ever-so-subtle *Earth energies* field, and perhaps more prominently in Hawai'i than anywhere else in the world. This is just one theory of why these areas of heightened energy and magnetism occur.

The islands formed millions of years ago when fountains of lava spewed up from volcanoes under the sea. Through the centuries, the lava built up underwater mountains and finally the tops of these mountains rose above the surface of the ocean, becoming the islands of the Hawaiian archipelago. In time the northwestern islands of the chain stopped erupting. They were eventually worn down by centuries of rain, wind, and wave, but the

islands of the southeastern part of the chain continued to erupt and grow.

When iron in liquid magma hardens, the magnetic field that exists at that particular place & time is "set in stone", creating a permanent magnetic signature in the lava rock. Solidified lava and magnetism in rock samples from Hawai'i's early formation might contain a different magnetic signature than freshly hardened lava from today, creating a clash of different polarities.

The building process of Paradise, accompanied by an occasional earthquake, continues on the island of Hawai'i, the largest of the island group. The Big Island has multiple active volcanoes, and the Big Island is larger than all other islands combined. There are five majestic volcanoes total comprising the Big Island: Mauna Kea, Mauna Loa, Kilauea, Kohala, and Hualalai. An underwater volcano, named Loihi, is said to be rising from the ocean floor just southeast of the island. Interestingly enough, there are stories of malfunctioning equipment by fisherman in that area.

Another theory about vortex formation has to do with what's called "reduced binding", a peculiar phenomenon that was studied intensely by the US Navy and the Canadian National Research Council near Lake Ontario during the 1950's. Invisible columns of swirling magnetism, some up to 1000 feet in diameter, were measured and in 2001 magnetic and gravitational data obtained by satellites actually suggested a lessening of the grip of gravity in the area. The atmosphere of earth is continually building up electrical differentials and discharging electrical potential. The earth itself has electrical currents. Deposits of quartz crystal are piezoelectric, that is, they generate electricity under pressure. Striking two pieces of quartz together creates a spark. Ions in the air from sources such as waterfalls also contribute to the overall electrical field.

Coincidentally, you tend to find structures like pyramids, standing stones, megaliths or heiaus at, on or near these energetically charged locations, perhaps as a testament to ancient people's ability to sense such energy.

Many individuals have studied the Earth Energy Field. Historian *Nikolai Goncharov*, construction engineer *Vyacheslav Morozov* and electronics specialist *Valery Makarov* were a team of Russian researchers who detected a geometric grid pattern interlinking a wide number of natural phenomena, all establishing a single planetary energy system.

A continuous interaction is believed to take place among the Earth's major and minor vortexes through an "Earth Energy Field". It is described as a matrix of connective pathways resembling the human circulatory, nervous, or acupuncture meridian systems. Their intersection culminates creating high energy vortexes. Some are deemed positive in nature and others negative. The Himalayas and the Peruvian Inca territories are considered Positive Vortexes. On the other hand, the Bermuda Triangle and the Devil's Sea, east of Japan, were identified as "Vile Vortexes" or "Electromagnetic Disturbances" by American biologist Ivan P. Sanderson. He discovered twelve negative energy Spots, caused by hot and cold currents, symmetrically distributed at equidistant

locations from the equator. Mapping those locations revealed an energetic network connecting them.

Likewise, Professors William Becker and Bethe Hagens followed Ivan T. Sanderson's results to chart an "Earth Energy Grid".

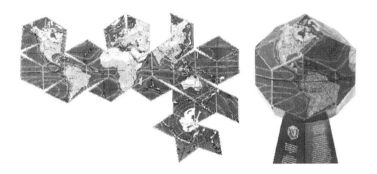

Becker stated:

"The Earth is really a living crystal being, with a geometric skeleton that could be mapped in its patterns of energy flows... in ocean currents, the winds, river systems, and distributions of precious minerals. It even seemed that ancient humans had known this sacred, hidden body of the Earth, and sited their civilizations to take advantage of her very visceral powers..."

The Becker-Hagen *Earthstar Globe*, a crystal shaped globe consisting of 30 equal-sided diamonds, features these 12 vile vortex locations as the twelve equatorial points on a sphere. When laid flat the globe shows the earth in very accurate proportion. When fully assembled, the globe shows the Hamakulia vortex as one of the protruding corners, the same with eleven other points on the map, including the Bermuda Triangle.

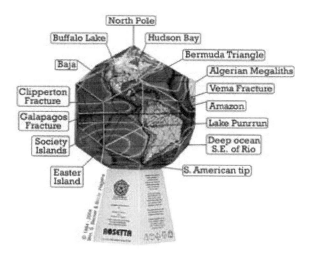

An actual consumer-available foldable model, the Earthstar globe embodies the Becker-Hagen planetary grid theory. Becker and Hagen also wrote: "*Our goal in producing Earthstar was the creation of*

a map that would be comfortable to an audience oriented to the equatorial linearity and continental positioning of a standard Mercator map." The Earthstar's underlying geometry is the "rhombic triacontahedron" projection method developed by R. Buckminster Fuller."

The entire list of twelve Vile Vortexes is as follows:

The Bermuda Triangle
Hamakulia, northeast of Hawaii Island
Japan's Devil's Sea
Off the coast of Rio de Janeiro, Brazil
Wharton Basin, in the Indian Ocean
Algeria's Megalithic Ruins
Pakistan's Lower Indus Valley
Easter Island Megaliths
Loyalty Islands, New Caledonia
Great Zimbabwe
North and South Poles

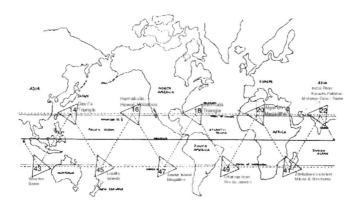

You've probably heard of the Bermuda Triangle, am I right? The world famous triangle is just one of the vile vortices that appear across the planet, and according to Sanderson, there's another one just northeast of Hawai'i too, known as *Hamakulia*, the final vortex I researched for this guide book.

The term "vile vortices" was coined in 1972 by Ivan Sanderson, in an article he wrote for *Saga* Magazine called "*The Twelve Devil's Graveyards from Around the World*", where he described certain zones of anomalous activity that were set apart at 72-degree intervals latitudinal, areas where strong air currents swirled and warmer surface temps from the tropics met with colder waters of the temperate zones. These conditions produced extreme temperature variables and the potential for air or marine disturbances. Sanderson theorized that ships and planes could somehow move into a vortex, where a series of effects would be triggered, setting off natural phenomena that might result in magnetic or electronic "gymnastics" of sorts, which just might sink a ship or down a plane.

Vile or not, these sites deserve more attention than they are currently receiving. The relationship between the earth and us has always been reciprocal: we are connected through an omnipresent universal energy. Unfortunately, our modern economy and the wide spread pollution have contaminated the planet. As the dominant conscious species on this planet, it is our duty to keep a healthy energetic flow by synchronizing our lifestyles to her rhythm and create a harmonious habitat for ourselves and other sentient beings.

Over a period of approximately 26,000 years, the earth's North Pole moves through a succession of "North Stars." This motion is also called the Precession of the Equinox. As the earth neared the point of greatest inclination to the sun (December 21, 2012), more extreme weather began to affect the earth, since the sun drives the jet stream. I wrote about this in detail in my first book, *Pyramid Rising: Planetary Acupuncture to Combat Climate Change.* The sun is subject to short-term and long-term cycles, storms, and flares, known as solar minimums/maximums. The electro-magnetic fields of the sun and the earth are inextricable from one

another. As an earthling, your cellular and body's electromagnetic fields (your aura) are also inseparable from the sun's and the earth's energies.

The earth's dynamic magnetic field lines at the poles receive more charged solar particles that at the magnetic "equator." These solar particles light up the atmosphere in the spectacular Aurora Borealis (Northern Lights) and Aurora Australis (Southern Lights). The earth's magnetic field is not stable; Magnetic North Pole wanders and periodically (over tens and hundreds of thousands of years) the polarity reverses. This is proven by magnetic patterns remaining recorded in lava flows, which is how geologists date the age of Hawai'i. As the magma cools and hardens, it aligns magnetically.

The influence of the sun, the influence of the molten core, and to a lesser extent the local surface features and mineral deposits contribute to the overall magnetic field. Especially where ancient deposits are exposed by surface erosion, local electromagnetic fields will be different from the surrounding "over-all" field. Such magnetic anomalies

are mapped on sectional air charts to assist pilots, who formerly relied on magnetic compass.

Whenever you have strong magnetism present within the landscape, you have to be somewhat cautious when flying a plane or sailing a ship. Electronics might be affected by the variations in magnetism and equipment may even malfunction. Aeronautical maps include areas that register as highly magnetic, just so pilots know to steer clear of the energetic area. There are two graphics in this book that show strong magnetic disturbances near Mauna Loa and Kilauea.

Certain vortexes are more intense than others, and they can affect animals and people too. Animals that rely on earth magnetism for migration are more easily susceptible to disturbances, such as whales, dolphins, and birds to name a few. This fact makes you wonder about animals whose "internal compasses" may get interrupted, often leading to beachings and other animal related events like mass bird deaths. Also makes you wonder if these magnetic anomalies affect humans too? Maybe after

you visit a few of the vortexes mentioned in this field guide, you will come to believe they do.

Identifying Vortexes

Vortexes typically exist where there are strong concentrations of gravitational anomalies, in turn creating an environment that can defy gravity, bend light, scare animals, twist plant life into contorted shapes, and cause humans to feel strange.

Many vortexes have been shown to be associated with Ley Lines and have been found to be extremely strong at node points where the lines cross. Worldwide, the Great Pyramid in Egypt and Stonehenge in England are perhaps the most well known as centers of vortex activity. Often overlooked, not known, or discounted as vortex influences, but equally as powerful and fully interrelated in the overall scheme of things, are **Human Body Vortexes** and **Sun Vortexes**.

This chapter offers some techniques for discovering vortexes by observing animals, plants, sounds, intuition and by studying maps and aerial photographs.

Vortexes can appear in many forms, large and small, spherical, angular, comprised of various forms of energies. Different Vortexes are detected by different methods. Common visible Vortexes such as water spouts, dust devils, tornadoes, and hurricanes have spiraling energies that manifest physical signs of their passing and typically leave evidence of their powerful force. Other types of energy Vortexes are often elusive and don't create or leave physical signs of their existence. Let's look at the definition of "vortex" a little further.

The *Oxford Dictionary* definition of the word vortex is:

"*A mass of whirling fluid or air, especially a whirlpool or whirlwind*". Another dictionary describes it as "*a place or situation regarded as drawing into its center all that surrounds it.*"

In other words, a vortex is a site where the energy of an area is concentrated to one central focal point. Draw a spiral from the outside in, and that would be the basic shape the energy of a vortex flows. A vortex in the *terrestrial* sense is considered a place in the landscape where the *earth energies* are

distinct from the energies in the surrounding area. *Earth energy* loosely refers to the physical forces of Nature that include gravity, magnetism, electricity, heat, light and sound. Here we are primarily interested in energies of the Earth, collectively called *geophysical energies*, which manifest as Vortexes and other magnetic anomalies.

Vortexes can often be identified by observing plants and animals, and because plants are influenced by vortex energies, the circular nature of vortexes can also be witnessed in aerial photos. Vortex energies seem to influence the course of rivers and mountain valleys. Like human faces, each vortex is distinct, but they share a common structure. Some vortexes are developed into tourist attractions, like those in Montana and Oregon, while others are undeveloped and even undiscovered.

Interestingly, the ancient symbol for a vortex is a *cross inside a circle* (see table of contents) which is extremely similar to the *swastika* symbol found in the artwork of many different nations.

The swastika symbol resembles a spinning vortex. Earth energies existed in ancient times, and were used by our ancestors for agricultural purposes as the energies increase crop production and fertility rates.

Most renditions of this symbol do not include a circle, however both Celtic & Japanese versions do show one. ***Is there a connection between vortex energy and the 12,000 year old swastika symbol?*** What do you think? Does a swastika look like a spinning vortex to you? Hopefully your perception of

this ancient symbol is changing into a more positive one, as it should be. It is a very ancient, sacred symbol found all across the world.

Vortexes are said to contain an abundance of geophysical energies that can either have a positive or negative effect on the environment and on people and animals. The positive, healing vortexes are usually identified as sacred; the negative ones, vile.

These vortexes are difficult to substantiate since they cannot be seen, but they are often felt by sensitives, psychics and many thousands of visitors each year. Scientists and researchers can now understand these energies by detecting them with precision equipment, such as a magnetometer, magnetic gradiometer, and even a simple device like a dowsing rod or pendulum. Using a magnetic gradiometer, researcher Pierre Mereux found that stone structures can actually impact the natural energies of the landscape, and small differences in earth current were detected inside and outside of certain rock chambers.

Many vortexes and sacred sites have already been identified and plotted by those in a previous

age, by an ancient civilization that existed during a time when constructing with stone and marking certain special points in the landscape was the thing to do. Around the globe, researchers today are concluding that they aren't the first ones to be able to detect these energetic sites, and modern science is finally just beginning to acknowledge and understand them.

Further research into these mysteries has led many to find that certain vortex sites are connected by invisible lines of energy, known by scientists as telluric currents and often dubbed "ley-lines" by vortex enthusiasts and researchers alike.

According to authors Pete A. Sanders Jr. and Richard Dannelley in their works *"Scientific Vortex Information"* and *"Sedona Power Spot Vortex"*, vortexes are labeled according to the direction of their energy flow: Up-flow vortexes, where energy is flowing upward out of the earth, and Inflow vortexes, where energy is flowing inward, toward the earth. Up-flow vortexes are said to boost spiritual skills associated with going to a higher level. They are said to stretch or expand consciousness, like filling a

balloon with air. Places labeled as a *magnetic vortex* are areas of inflow energy. An area labeled an *electric vortex* is an area of up-flow energy.

Sometimes vortexes are referred to as 'positive' or 'negative.' The terms are intended to be used more in a yin/yang fashion, meaning neither good nor bad, just being opposite. However, there are those that feel there actually are 'negative vortexes' in the sense of meaning bad or evil. Such a conception is not true. It is thought the misconception originated when Up-flow vortexes were labeled 'positive' because of the tremendous exhilaration they generated. While an experience at an Up-flow vortex is exhilarating, an inflow area generates a much more pensive feeling. Because the power of the vortex is flowing down rather than up, the energy at an inflow site feels heavier. On a spiritual quest or during introspective exploration, if not prepared, the first things people experience is confusion. As a result inflow areas are often thought of as negative or evil.

Animals

Of all animals, cats seem most apprehensive, if not completely adamant about not wanting to venture into some vortexes. Dogs normally don't have a problem accompanying their owners into the vortex, but in many cases people notice strange behavior in their pets, such as his eyes following movement the rest of us don't see.

Large animals such as horses and deer are especially unwilling to cross into some vortexes, and deer will make trails that deliberately skirt the area even though it would seem to make more sense to go through it. Birds will often fly into the vortex, land, look around as if lost, and then finally leave without looking for bugs or worms. Cold-blooded animals like snakes or frogs, and insects have no problem with the area.

Patterns in Plant Growth

All bonafide mystery spots have a subtle and sometimes an overt affect on vegetation. Trees grow in anomalous ways, for example left-hand

(counterclockwise) spiraling of trunks, limbs grow along the lines of force, and rare plants are often found in the area. Because plants are influenced by vortex energies, the circular shape of vortexes can be seen in air photos.

Water Spots and Mineral Deposits

There are persistent theories that ore deposits cause the vortex phenomenon. Vortexes often do have ore deposits and unusual geologic formations nearby, but if these cause the effects, the mechanism has never been scientifically established.

Sound

Paul Devereux, former editor of Ley Hunter Journal, measured anomalies in ultrasound frequencies at some sacred sites during his "Dragon Project." Some people say that the note B# (B-sharp) does not sound in tune at a vortex.

Unexplained Lights

Occasionally, visitors at vortexes photograph anomalies such as light balls (orbs) and light streaks. Film cameras can capture the "light streak", while digital cameras more often capture the "light ball."

Psychics & Sensitives

Over the years, I've met a lot of people who claim to have a special sensitivity to energy. I can pick it up at times, and I've heard that everyone has psychic abilities, just not everyone develops them. While most people have never paid attention to the subtle energies and sensations, sensitivity seems to come naturally to some, and apparently the skill can be acquired with practice.

Intuition

Tune in to your intuition in your own way for more information.

A vortex can be an area of concentrated energy that promotes a sense of well being

I am glad to know many individuals on the island who are gifted in this sense, who have joined me in the Kahuna Research Group where they share their gifts of healing and intuition with others.

Dowsing / Water Witching

For generations, well-drillers have relied on dowsing to site well, because it works. Dowsers often use a forked stick, or a pair of rods or a pendulum made of nearly any material. When dowsing rods are held loosely in the hands, parallel to the ground and to each other, the body responds to a change in the

electromagnetic field and the rods move. A pendulum swings either back and forth or in a circle. Techniques vary, according to each individual dowser, and this is of less importance than method and intent.

Everyone experiences vortexes differently. For example, some people experience a tingling sensation in parts of their body, other people feel a change in temperature, others just "know." At times even the sense of smell comes into play, even though some vortexes are located hundreds of miles from the ocean, at rare times the seashore can be smelled. Here in Hawai'i you shouldn't have to worry about that. Most days the warm tropical smell can be enjoyed from nearly anywhere on the island.

People occasionally report relief from various kinds of pain. Occasionally people feel slight dizziness or minor nausea, but don't worry, there are no lasting ill effects. Some people have claimed minor ailments cured in a "magic spot". Vortexes, however odd or bizarre, are natural phenomena, and they deserve more attention if you ask me. The human body is continually influenced by a stormy sea

of energies electromagnetic, gravity, and subtle energies, plus the "life" energy that goes by many different names, including chi, prana or orgone, and there are some locations where this energy is more condensed than others.

EMF Detector / Magnetometer

Most cell phones come with a magnetometer built in for the GPS feature which acts like a compass and magnetic detector. They can actually detect the subtle changes in magnetism found at vortexes. I use the app by Smart Tools on my phone which was not free but comes with a neat bundle of other tools that you may find useful. Also, a regular old compass might be good to bring, to help locate each vortex.

Some tools I used when determining the sizes and strengths of the vortexes in this book are the **IOD40 Ion Detector, Mel Meter, Radiant Energy Probe**, different **pendulums** and the trusty **copper dowsing rods**.

IOD40 - Ion Field Detector

The IOD40 Ion Field Detector is a very versatile tool that detects both positive and negative electric fields produced by ions, electricity and ultra low static fields. This unit is sensitive enough to detect the minute charge produced by just rubbing a piece of plastic and bringing the probe in proximity. It easily measures the electric field during a thunder storm or other high static conditions long before the storm arrives. It has been observed that certain paranormal activity is often accompanied by a distortion of the electric field. These changing fields are usually too weak to be detected by conventional detectors.

The Radiant Energy Probe
Dubbed "*The Wand*". This device detects energy fields produced by electrical activity and other unknown anomalies. It uses *no*  *batteries* or other sources of power yet detects very weak and virtually unnoticed energy fields. It can also provide a three dimensional output "footprint" of medical healing machines such as Lakhovsky coils,

high voltage generators, ion machines, dangerous lightning levels, power line "e" field gradients, high frequency radiation from Tesla coils and other similar devices. This apparatus is **electrically balanced**.

While exploring the vortexes, I also used a Mel Meter that was specifically designed for anomalous research.

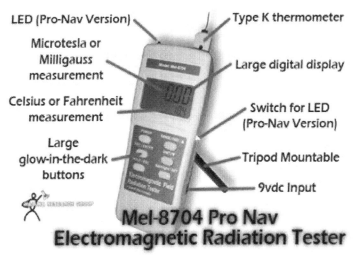

The Mel Meter measures small temperature changes and records EMF levels in both Microtesla and Milligauss format.

Well, enough about identifying vortexes, and time to start experiencing them. Over the next 12 chapters I detail each of the Big Island's energy vortex sites.

Mauna Kea Vortex

Vortex Type: Healing
Strength: Strong
Public Access: Yes
Fee: No
Attractions: Observatories, National Park, Ice Age Reserve, ancient stone quarry, hiking, sacred lake

Quick Fact: Measured from its submarine base (3,280 fathoms) to the peak (13,803 feet, or 4,207 meters, above sea level), Mauna Kea is the tallest mountain in the world.

How to Get There:

Distance from Kona: 63.9 mi north on Hwy 11 or Hawai'i Belt Road | Distance from Hilo: 43.2 mi north via Daniel K. Inouye Hwy (formerly Saddle Road).

The drive to get to Mauna Kea is fairly self-explanatory: drive towards the giant snowcapped mountain in the distance, the one with all the observatories on it. A 43 mile scenic drive takes you from sea level in Hilo or Kona up to the summit of Mauna Kea at an astonishing 13,796 feet.

This journey takes you through just about every ecosystem on the island. From the tropical rainforest atmosphere of Hilo on up through the 'Ohi'a forests of Saddle Road, (recently renamed the Daniel K. Inouye Highway), and then up the side of Mauna Kea, through ranch land and then up to the top, where little vegetation grows and the air is noticeably thinner.

Prepare yourself for a view of a lifetime! On a clear day you can see Maui and the neighboring islands as well as the active Pu'u O'o vent in Volcano.

View from near the top of Mauna Kea, with Mauna Loa in the distance. Notice the cluster of cinder cones, which could be due to the strong earth energies in the area.

Why it's sacred:

The whole mountain throughout history was used as a burial ground of the highest born and most sacred ancestors. And like the kupuna say, so many generations that they have turned to dust. But their spirit remains. In general, mountains have always been considered sacred, and in Hawai'i, giving life to so many in the middle of the vast Pacific Ocean, mountains are quite possibly more revered than anywhere else in the world. The tallest mountain in the entire Pacific, Mauna Kea, is still a rich repository of mythology and local lore. For this reason, it begins our tropical vortex adventure.

Since humans first arrived on the Hawaiian Islands, Mauna Kea, which translates to "White Mountain", has exerted a powerful divine magnetism and pilgrims have often made the long and arduous climb up its steep slopes.

The summits of the five volcanoes on the Big Island are highly respected, and Mauna Kea's summit, being the tallest, is considered the most

revered of all. For this reason, a Kapu (ancient Hawaiian law) restricted visitor rights to high ranking tribal chiefs.

Hawaiians associated elements of their natural environment with particular deities. In the local mythology, the sky father Wakea marries the earth mother Papa, giving birth to the Hawaiian Islands. In many of these genealogical myths, Mauna Kea is portrayed as the pair's first born son.

The summit of Mauna Kea is seen as the "region of the gods", a place where benevolent spirits reside. Poli'ahu, deity of snow, also resides there. Also known as an ancient vortex of the historic Lemurian culture, the Hawaiians always paid homage to Poli'ahu as they prayed for the rain waters to keep their crops green and communities fed. Ancient Hawaiians living on the slopes of Mauna Kea relied on its extensive forests for food, and quarried dense volcano-glacial basalts on its flanks for tool production – also strengthening the belief that this mountain was sacred, as it provided for the people in more ways than one.

Mauna Loa Vortex

Vortex Type: Healing
Strength: Strong
Public Access: Yes
Fee: No
Attractions: Mauna Loa Observatory, Mauna Loa Trail, Ainapo Trail, camping, hiking, ancient paved trails

Quick Fact: Mauna Loa is the largest active volcano in the world in terms of mass. It last erupted between March 23 – April 15, 1984.

How to get there: Even though Mauna Loa is closer to the southern tip of the island, you have to go north to get there. A 17-mile (one way) scenic drive, off of Saddle Road, takes you to Mauna Loa observatory and the next vortex on our list. Be warned, this hike is not for the faint of heart and requires a small degree of preparation.

In Hawaiian, Mauna Loa means "Long Mountain", and boy is that true! This volcano is a "shield volcano", or basaltic volcano, and unlike the Cascade volcanoes (andesitic volcanoes) shield volcanoes are rarely explosive and mostly just *ooze*.

Basalt is a type of lava that is very fluid when erupted. Therefore these types of volcanoes are not steep and are shaped just like a shield laid on the ground. The first Ancient Hawaiians to arrive on Hawaii Island lived along the shores where food and water were plentiful Flightless birds that had previously known no predators became a staple food source. Early settlements had a major impact on the local ecosystem, and caused much extinction, particularly amongst bird species, as well as introducing foreign plants and animals and increasing erosion rates. The prevailing lowland forest ecosystem was transformed from forest to grassland; some of this change was caused by the use of fire, but the main reason appears to have been the introduction of the Polynesian Rat (*Rattus exulans*).

Ancient Hawaiian religious practice holds that the five volcanic peaks of the island are sacred, and regards Mauna Loa, the largest of them all, with great admiration; but what mythology survives today consists mainly of oral accounts from the 18th century first compiled in the 19th. Most of these stories agree that the Hawaiian volcano deity, Pele,

resides in Halemaʻumaʻu Crater on Kilauea; however a few place her home at Mauna Loa's summit caldera Mokuʻāweoweo, and the mythos in general associates her with all volcanic activity on the island. Regardless, Kilauea's lack of a geographic outline and strong volcanic link to Mauna Loa led to it being considered an offshoot of Mauna Loa by the Ancient Hawaiians, meaning much of the mythos now associated with Kilauea was originally directed at Mauna Loa as well.

Ancient Hawaiians constructed an extensive trail system on Hawai'i Island, today known as the Ala Kahakai National Historic Trail. The network consisted of short trailheads servicing local areas along the main roads and more extensive networks within and around agricultural centers. The positioning of the trails were practical, connecting living areas to farms and ports and regions to resources, with a few upland sections reserved for gathering and most lines marked well enough to remain identifiable long after regular use has ended. One of these trails, the Ainapo Trail, ascended from

the village of Kapapala over 3,400 m (11,155 ft) in about 56 km (35 mi) and ended at Mokuʻaweoweo at Mauna Loa's summit. Although the journey was arduous and required several days and many porters, ancient Hawaiians likely made the journey during eruptions to leave offerings and prayers to honor Pele, much as they did at Halemaʻumaʻu, neighboring Kilauea's more active and more easily accessible caldera. Several camps established along the way supplied water and food for travelers.

Why it's Sacred:

Mauna Loa is situated near the notorious 19.5° degrees north of the Equator mark, another reason to include it in this book. 19.5° is the angle that's been found by researchers to be repeatedly encoded in certain structures on not only the Earth, but all planets in our solar system, and even the sun, where sunspots form.

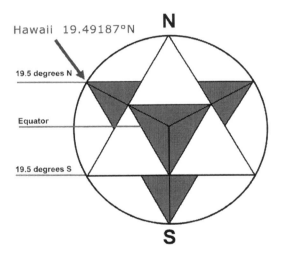

Hawaii falls on the 19.5 degree mark.

The apexes of a tetrahedron, when placed within a circumscribing sphere, one of the tetrahedron's apexes touching the North Pole, the other three apexes touch the surface of the sphere at

-9.5 degrees south latitude. The mark has been found to be associated with various ancient structures here on Earth – The Giza pyramids, Avebury stone circle, Pyramids of the Sun and Moon at Teotihuacan, and more.

Spirituality is an important part of Hawaiian culture. There is a wide range of stories and legends that families have passed down over the years. The two major volcanoes on the Big Island --Mauna Loa and Kilauea-- are the source of many colorful stories, not to mention active lava flows.

This air chart shows a magnetic disturbance of "as much as 8 degrees" in the area near Mauna Loa.

The summit of Mauna Loa is where the goddess Pele found refuge. Hawaiian legends say that volcano goddess Pele was driven from her home by her angry older sister, Na-maka-o-kaha'i because Pele had seduced her husband. Every time Pele would thrust her digging stick into the earth to dig a pit for a new home, *Na-maka-o-kaha'i*, goddess of water and the sea, would flood the pits. Pele eventually landed on the Big Island, where she made Mauna Loa her new home. Mauna Loa was so tall that even Pele's sister could not send the ocean's waves high enough to drown Pele's fires. So Pele established her home on its slopes, and establishing Mauna Loa as one of Hawai'i's most sacred sites.

Curiously, it has also been observed that 19.5° degrees is closely linked, for some reason, with certain NASA space missions. For example, *Mars Pathfinder* landed at 19.5° degrees lat. of Mars on July 4, '97.

Travel Notes:

Kilauea Vortex

Vortex Type: Healing
Strength: Strong
Public Access: Yes
Fee: Yes
Attractions: Volcanoes National Park, Halema'uma'u Crater, Crater Rim drive, Kilauea iki Crater, Thurston Lava Tube, Volcano House, hiking, camping

Quick Fact: At present, Kilauea volcano is still having one of the most long-lived eruptions known on earth, which started in 1983 on the eastern rift zone and has mainly been concentrated at the Pu'u 'O'o vent.

How to get there:

Distance from Kona: 96 mi. south on Hwy 11 | Distance from Hilo: 30 mi

Enter this place with reverence, for you are in the mighty and magnificent dwelling place of the Goddess of Fire, Madame Pele, – one of the world's most active volcanoes!

Your first stop in Hawai'i Volcanoes National Park should be at the Kilauea Visitor Center where you'll find all the information you need in the form of brochures, maps, and informative park rangers. You can also watch a short film that introduces the park and get updates on volcanic activity. Become slightly familiar with the park before venturing out on your own, especially if you decide to do any hiking.

Most visitors to the island arrive in Kona International Airport (KOA) because there's daily direct flights from major international air carriers. The only bummer thing is is that Kona is about 2-1/2 to 3 hours from the National Park. Luckily for you, there are vortex destination all along the way. Your vortex expedition should be a fun, safe adventure, so you'll want to be as prepared as you can for your visit. Make sure you have a full tank of gas in your car before you start, and take along food and water. If you can, stop at a local fruit or coffee stand to experience how fresh the island really is.

Dress in appropriate hiking clothes and stay on marked routes only, for your safety above all else.

Keep your eye open for that Kodak moment, and capture it. Pay attention to all signs and information plaques, you just might learning something you've never heard before. Again, you can find out all important safety and volcanic activity information at the Visitor Center.

For the best experience possible, bring binoculars, a flashlight, and your camera, of course. If your phone has a magnetometer app, consider taking a reading of your own to detect any heightened levels of magnetism. If you detect something anomalous such as a spike in magnetism, detect how it makes you feel. If you feel good, then perhaps rest and meditate. If it feels awkward consider moving on to the next spot. If you're determined to see live lava flows, plan your trip so that you are well into the trail at dawn or dusk when the lava is most visible.

Why it's Sacred:

This volcano has been shrouded in myth and legend since the dawn of time. A continuous swirl of

volcanic magma makes for one powerful vortex. You don't need to take a reading with some fancy detector to know that!

An active volcano is what makes the vortex energy here so powerful, acting as a doorway for the northern hemisphere consistently held open by forces beyond explanation.

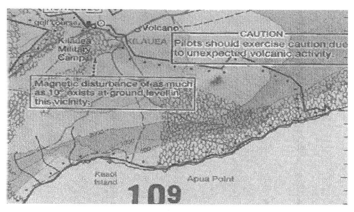

This air chart shows a magnetic disturbance of "as much as 10 degrees" in the area near Kilauea.

Home to the gods, such as "Madame Pele", this island vortex is sure to make a lasting impression. *Pele* is as much revered for her beauty as she is feared for her anger, which is said to manifest itself as volcanic quakes and eruptions. The

daughter of deities *Haumea* and *Kane-hoa-lani*, Pele is said to live in Kilauea Crater and her life and exploits are well-known within local folklore.

She is also fond of walking among mortals, appearing in guises that include vanishing hitchhikers, beautiful maidens, and even old women. She often appears unexpectedly in photographs taken all over the islands. Snap a few shots when visiting and maybe you'll be lucky enough to see something. If not there are further telltale signs of her presence, if you just look down. On the ground you might be able to see what's called "Pele's Hair", an actual geological term for small wispy fragments of volcanic glass threads or fibers formed when small particles of molten material are thrown into the air and spun out by the wind into long hair-like strands.

An example of "Pele's Hair" – Volcanic Glass Fibers

These strands were collected to make fishing hooks and other tools used by the Hawaiians. Another way the land brought forth life to the Hawaiians, who are still devoted deeply to nature, the *aina*.

Pele's temper is so respected that locals will often admonish tourists to refrain from bringing volcanic rocks off the islands. It's said that doing so will incur her wrath, and unless the rocks are returned, their holders will have catastrophic bad luck. Even though the late park ranger Narou Tovley of Hawai'i Volcanoes National Park claimed to have made up the story to preserve the natural environment, locals still adhere to the ages-old warning. Lava rocks to this day are shipped back to the Islands from tourists who claimed to have suffered from Madame Pele's curse.

Although there are five total volcanoes on the Big Island, only three are active in a geological sense. Mount Hualalai is one, which last erupted over 200 years ago and the second is Mauna Loa, whose last eruption was in 1984. However, our current

vortex location Mt. Kilauea has been erupting continuously since 1983.

The Volcanoes of the Hawaiian Island chain normally create gentle eruption cycles that do not have the violence associated with them, as was witnessed in the cataclysmic eruption of Mount Saint Helens in 1980. As a consequence, the eruptions of this usually slow flowing, ropey-type of lava, are relatively safe to view, as well as being scenic and spectacular, especially when viewed at a safe distance at night or from offshore. Kilauea's eruption is one of the most beautiful and visceral attractions that you will ever see. It's not often that you will have the opportunity to visit an active, erupting volcano and no one knows when Kilauea will stop its current flow. Hawaii Volcanoes National Park is undoubtedly Hawai'i Island's best attraction, and it is also the only *World Heritage* destination on the island. It can be enjoyed year round and sometimes even overnight, which is the perfect time when you are able to see the glowing red of the active lava flows against the night sky.

Travel Notes:

Kalani Vortex

Vortex Type: Healing
Strength: Moderate
Public Access: Yes
Fee: Yes
Attractions: Kalani Oceanside Retreat, trails, heiau, halau

Quick Fact: Kalani is Hawai'i's largest retreat center, one of the best-loved centers in the world for more than 35 years.

How to Get There:
Distance from Kona: 107.6 miles | Distance from Hilo: 34.2 miles

This power spot is only a 45 minute drive from the Hilo airport and approximately 2.5hrs from Kona. There is public transportation via the Hele-On county bus that leaves from downtown Hilo. The bus goes right to Kalani if you can coordinate schedules. For detailed driving directions, Kalani Oceanside Retreat has provided a directional PDF.

Visitors to this sacred site often share stories about finding new and creative direction, and some

people experience sudden, unexpected bursts of emotion, according to the retreat's guestbook. Visitors to this vortex are encouraged to stay overnight to allow optimal experience.

Why it's Sacred:

Teacher and frequent visitor to Kalani, White Eagle Medicine Woman, often spoke to large audiences about how she felt guided to build a community drum there. She refers to Hawai'i as the *heart chakra*, or heart center, of the planet, Alaska as the crown and Macchu Picchu in Peru as the root. White Eagle's prophecy is that *"Kalani and the Big Island have a bigger role in shifting mass consciousness for change, setting the energy of intention through a powerful global grid"*, according to the retreat's blog. (See references for link)

The Big Island may not be as famous for sacred geography, but clearly it has a powerful position to hold amongst its well known cousins. There is no doubt that those who visit again and again will confidently declare Kalani and the Big

Island as a whole a major "power spot" for finding direction and creating new dreams.

At Kalani Oceanside Retreat Village three important heritage sites are open for visitors to experience in reverence, led by Hawaiian cultural practitioners at Kalani. A heiau temple site and a halau school site, plus Ala Kai coastal trail sections, some over 500 years old, are all preserved and registered with the Hawai'i State Department of Land and Natural Resources.

The heiau has been re-consecrated by native kahuna spiritual leaders, and is dedicated to Lono and Kanaloa, gods of agricultural and ocean abundance, peace, parties, and prosperity. The halau operated until 1900 and transitioned from a traditional thatched structure housing teachings in native cultural practices to the inclusion of western missionary influenced learning.

On the following page you can see a picture of the heiau as it was missed by a lava flow. Did

some kind of vortex energy prevent this temple from being covered with lava?

A few native burial grounds are also viewable along the beautiful Kalapana-Kapoho Beach Road (Highway 137), however most are hidden and protected on private properties, and should not be sought out, viewed or disturbed.

Punalu'u Vortex

Vortex Type: Healing
Strength: Mild
Public Access: Yes
Fee: No
Attractions: Black sand, sea turtles, swimming, small tourist shop, freshwater spring and pond, trail hiking, historic sites, vacation rentals, golf course

Quick Fact: Punalu'u Black Sand Beach is the largest black sand beach in the state. The beach is mostly made of hematite and magnetite, and the pebbles are magnetic.

How to Get There:
Distance from Kona: 67 miles south | Distance from Hilo: 58 miles south on Hwy. 11

Of all the black sand beaches on the island, Punalu'u is probably the most famous of the bunch. As soon as you arrive you will see why. On a perfect day, a golden glow can be seen from the beach, making me think of small concentrations of minerals in the sand. A freshwater underground spring emerges from just off shore, making the water here noticeably cooler and different. There's also a freshwater pond home to ducks and many other

forms of wildlife, complete with a walking path and bridge.

The black sand at this beach is magnetic, consisting of magnetite and hematite among other things, and marks the next vortex on our list. Most of the Vortexes in Hawai'i are the healing kind, and it's my hope that you conclude the same.

A spiral rock formation at Punalu'u Black Sand Beach. You can see this formation on Google Earth.

Why it's Sacred:

Green sea turtles enjoy swimming and foraging here, and can often be seen warming

themselves on the beach. Turtles are considered sacred, as the earth itself is believed by Hawaiians to be resting on the back of a Cosmic Turtle. As the numerous signs say, please don't touch them, but you can definitely get close enough to get a great photo without disturbing them at all. The beach itself isn't very long but there's always a nice place to hang out next to the lagoon which also connects to the beach. Watch for falling fronds (leaves) and coconuts from the palm trees that line the beach as you find a spot to sit. Lifeguards are usually staffed here but not always, so take that into consideration if you go swimming. The ocean currents can get fairly strong here, but if you get a particular call to swim, the water is very pure. You won't regret it.

A Honu (sea turtle) taking a break on the warm sandy beach.

It's my belief that the magnetic sand and freshwater spring has a beneficial healing effect, giving me a reason to include it on the list. Stay as long as you want at this wonderful and unique destination. There's even a rental house on the beach that might be available if you decide to stay the night.

South Point Vortex

Vortex Type: Healing
Strength: Moderate
Public Access: Yes
Fee: No
Attractions: Ka lae Nat'l Historic Landmark, Heiau o Kalalea, ancient canoe moorings, southernmost point in the USA, green sand beach, cliff jumping

Quick Fact: Ka Lae is the southernmost point in the U.S. and is believed to be the point where the ancient Polynesians first landed on Hawai'i.

How to Get There:
Distance from Kona: 63.4 miles south | Distance from Hilo: 79.8 miles south on Hwy. 11

The South Point vortex is located at the end of a relatively straight 12 mile road, and offers you some breathtaking scenery along the way. A short ways after the road turns from paved to gravel you can park next to high cliffs to the right, or keep left on to the second parking lot.

At the first parking area, you can almost always find parking as this is a major attraction on

cur island. Take a picture! You are literally standing on the official southernmost point in the US. This is the exact place where the first Polynesians arrived to the islands. Not a bad place to pull up to Paradise.

If you continue forward past the first lot you will reach the second parking lot at the trailhead to the green sand beach. The 2.25 mile hike to the natural Olivine beach takes about 45 minutes each direction and sturdy shoes are highly recommended. There are usually rides available from the locals, making for a one of a kind experience, usually in the back of a 4x4 truck.

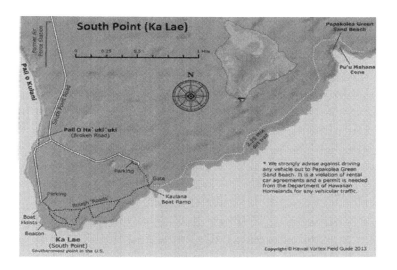

I personally recommend walking along the coastline if you're not in a rush. Just keep following the coast until you eventually come to a small peak, you can't miss it. Chances are you run in to other adventurers. Prepare to get dusty if you walk in the 4x4 tracks, if that bothers you keep an eye open for a grass or rock trail. There are walking trails marked out by years of determined visitors, but it's easy to miss them as there are literally dozens of different paths to get there.

The scenery here is nothing short of spectacular, and the green sand beach that awaits you has great waves for boogie or body boarding. Open endless fields, crashing ocean swells, peculiar atmosphere, and the occasional bird or two can be expected. The entire area has a unique energy to it and it's been said that the locals are affected by it, often needing to remain barefoot just to stay grounded.

Why it's Sacred:

It is believed that the first Polynesians to arrive in the Hawaiian Islands disembarked here at

Ka Lae somewhere between 400 and 800 A.D. With the ruins of heiau (temples), fishing shrines and other cultural vestiges found here it's no wonder why this entire southern tip has been registered as a National Historical Landmark.

Travel to the southern cliffs of Hawaii Island in the Ka'u region and gaze out at the endless Pacific Ocean. Can you believe there's nothing but deep-blue ocean between the spot you're standing on and Antarctica? That's because you're at Ka Lae, also known as South Point or simply "The Point," the southernmost point in the United States.

The offshore currents and winds are notoriously powerful here and mariners from the first Polynesians to today's locals have devised clever ways of plying the rich fishing grounds without being swept away. For instance, you'll find rock loops carved through the lava here that tied off fishing canoes hundreds of years ago. Today, shoreline fishermen use toy boats to haul their lines into deep water or large metal boat hoists and ladders to launch small watercraft. The actual point is a short

walk away in front of the black-and-white light beacon, where there are no cliffs.

To get to this rocky shoreline you need to take the narrow South Point Road 12-miles through open ranch lands lined with white windmills. There is a small heiau (sacred place of worship) near Ka Lae so visitors should treat the area with great respect. Because of the dangerous currents here, swimming is not advised.

Besides being the landing place of the first Hawaiians, and home to a remarkable green sand beach, South Point, known locally as *Ka lae*, is said by the local residents to be like a rift in time. UFO sightings and intense energies are things you may hear about taking place there. The ley line coming into the South Point vortex of the Big Island, not far from Kalani, is considered to be one of the most powerful to be on land. Author William "Pila" Chiles talks about the South Point as a "doorway" where "the density of three dimensional reality seems to be very thin" and the energy is "very unusual".

The South Point vortex is believed to be an aperture or 'doorway' between dimensions, one of many to exist in the world. It's our belief after researching and writing this book that Hawai'i is connected in some ways to India as well as Egypt, two other sacred locations, by what is referred to as the World Grid.

Is there any evidence that Hawai'i is somehow connected with these faraway lands, or rather, that the ancient cultures of the world perhaps originated from one common place (Mu?). It depends on who you ask I suppose, but that's a different story.

Place of Refuge Vortex

Vortex Type: Healing
Strength: Moderate
Public Access: Yes
Fee: Yes
Attractions: Pu'uhonua o honaunau Nat'l Historic Park, swimming, picnic area

Quick Fact: Pu'uhonua O Honaunau is the most famous and well preserved of Hawai'i's ancient places of refuge.

How to Get There:
Distance from Kona: 22.4 miles south | Distance from Hilo: 98.4 miles

This vortex is the perfect setting for people who need to relax and take a load off from their daily routine. A place to sit and absorb all that really is. Many people who make the sojourn here have reported feeling a complete sense of renewal that only comes with curative Vortexes.

When you arrive to the Pu'uhonua o Honaunau National Park, which opens at 7AM, you

will have to pay the $5 entrance fee to get in. After talking with the park attendant and paying the toll, be sure to grab a park brochure. This will help you on your tour. Keep in mind the ticket is good for one week should you decide to come back again.

The official closing time at the park is 5PM, but you are allowed to remain on the grounds until sunset. The Visitor Center is open from 8:30 AM - 4:30 PM daily.

Zach visiting Ale'ale'a Heiau, the principle heiau of the Place of Refuge.

There are said to be two distinct energies that you might notice while in the park, calming nurturing energy, and intense built-up emotional energy.

According to numerous eyewitnesses, certain phenomena are said to have occurred here, including ball of light apparitions and gigantic 30 foot tall specters! According to some legends, giants were said to have lived on the island, and some ancient Hawaiians were said to be nearly 8 feet tall. Once inside the park, pause and take a deep breath, centering yourself. Notice how different this vortex is than any other ones we've visited already. A feeling of tranquility and peace floats on the gentle breeze.

Can you feel it, too?

Why it's Sacred:

Imagine you had just broken one of the ancient sacred laws, known as the *"Kapu"*, and the ensuing punishment was death. Your only chance of survival is to escape your pursuers and reach the *Pu'uhonua*, a place of refuge.

The *Pu'uhonua* sanctuary protected the ancient law breaker and even defeated warriors during the time of war; so that no harm could come to those who reached the inside of the safe haven. If

you reached this sacred place, your life would be spared. The offender would eventually be absolved by a priest and cleared to leave the shelter, back to normal life. These people were given a second chance at life itself. This was not a place teeming with hardened criminals. This was a sacred place on which a new life began. The Kapu laws were abolished in 1819.

As you enter notice the great wall that rises up marking the boundaries between the royal grounds and the sanctuary. Many *ki'i* (carved wooden images) surround the *Hale o Keawe*, housing the bones of the chiefs that infuse the area with their power or *mana*. The Pu'uhonua is still considered a sacred site. Please help to preserve the Pu'uhonua as in the ancient times. The *Ale'ale'a Heiau* at right was built in seven stages, and is a reminder how well ancient stonework survives. This heiau grounds the strong vortex energy here.

Paleaku Vortex

Vortex Type: Healing
Strength: Strong
Public Access: Yes
Fee: Yes
Attractions: Galaxy Garden, Native American medicine & fire wheels, labyrinth, Baha'i star, multi-denominational shrines, sand mandalas, library, yoga studio, vast gardens, meditation & shrine room, meeting hall, petroglyphs. **Open Tues–Sat 9am-4pm**

Quick Fact: Paleaku Peace Gardens was one of 10 locations worldwide to receive a live uplink to NASA's website for the MARS landing of Curiosity.

How to Get There:
South from Kona on Highway 11 to Napoopoo Rd, above Kealakekua Bay. Continue to Middle Keei Rd and on to Painted Church Road. Follow the windy road until you see the sign for the sanctuary.

The Paleaku Peace Garden Sanctuary is a non-profit organization and one of my favorite places to connect with on the entire island, and though it didn't make the first edit of this book as an entire

chapter, I am very happy to include it now. This place is simply spectacular!

Quietly situated directly in the middle between Kealakekua Bay and Pu'uhonua o Honaunau National Historic Park (yes, I actually measured it) the gardens embody deep spiritual mana combined with amazing natural beauty that invites contemplation and creative expression.

Not only are there 800 year old petroglyphs inside a sacred cave, there are an abundance of *earth energies* here.

Why it's Sacred:

The Paleaku Garden's mission from day one has always been to create a strong sense of peace and harmony through beauty and balance. Rare flowers and trees share the space with macadamia nut, coffee and citrus orchards, along with more exotic fruit trees planted here from seeds brought in from around the globe. Meandering through the gate to the picture-perfect, manicured grounds, visitors are greeted with serendipitous ocean and coastal vistas

stretching from our last destination, the Place of Refuge, to Kealakekua Bay, the next stop on our list.

A vortex inspired floral arrangement at the Paleaku Peace Garden in South Kona. A vortex within a vortex! Visit Paleaku.com for more information or to plan a visit. Image by Pierre & Heidy Lesage.

The gently sloping terrain and beautifully manicured pathways provide easy access to the gardens, grottoes and the numerous shrines representing all the world's major religions, including Buddhism, Hinduism, Taoism, Islam, Christianity, Judaism, Native American, Baha'i Faith and Native Hawaiian. All were designed and built traditionally under the direction of kahuna, learned scholars, Tibetan priests, visiting swamis and local friends of the sanctuary.

All these religions touch each other in some way, creating a "sacred geometry" or Feng Shui. The creators of the garden stressed the fact that it was to be absolutely non-sectarian, a spiritual rather than religious center. The inclusion of a large walking labyrinth dating back to "pre-Christian" times is another testament to the respect and balance of beliefs exemplified at the gardens.

If you haven't noticed by now, I'm leaving each chapter short and sweet. It's up to you to finish writing each chapter, using your visit and experiences as the material. Paleaku Peace Garden is a great place to start.  A year pass runs about $100 last time I checked, and a day pass is $10 for visitors and $7 for residents. Maybe we'll see each other there, I like to frequent this place the most as it's usually "on the way" to where I'm going, both literally, and figuratively. See the back of the book for a free ticket for the gardens,

Kealakekua Bay Vortex

Vortex Type: Healing
Strength: Moderate
Public Access: Yes
Fee: No
Attractions: Captain Cook monument, Hikiau heiau, swimming, kayak rentals, wild dolphins

Quick Fact: Kealakekua Bay is the largest deep water bay in Hawai'i. It is also one of the most scenic areas on the Kona coast.

How to Get There:
Distance from Kona: 16.6 miles south| Distance from Hilo: 92.6 miles via Daniel K. Inouye Hwy.

Kealakekua Bay is located on the Kona coast of the island of Hawai'i about 16miles south of Kailua-Kona. Settled over a thousand years ago, the surrounding area contains many archeological and historical sites such as religious temples, and was listed in the National Register of Historic Places listings on the island of Hawai'i in 1973 as the Kealakekua Bay Historical District. The bay is a

marine life conservation district, a popular destination for kayaking, scuba diving and snorkeling.

Why it's Sacred:

Located here is the Hikiau Heiau, an ancient Hawaiian temple site that was built by King Kalani'opu'u. It is a *luakini* (human sacrifice) heiau. The original heiau used to be more than 250 feet long and 100 feet wide. A smaller stone platform is built on top of the main platform and is believed to have been the location of the *lele* (altar).

Hikiau Heiau at Kealakekua Bay

Hikiau Heiau was visited by Captain James Cook in 1778-1779. When the natives first saw his huge ship sail into Kealakekua Bay, they thought he was the returning god Lono, the god of agriculture and prosperity. The time when Cook arrived was during the months of the *makahiki*, which was a festival honoring the god Lono with hula performances, competitive games, feasting and special offerings.

Cook was treated as a divine guest by the Hawaiians. He attended a special ceremony at another nearby heiau that was held in his honor. And at Hikiau Heiau, he performed the first Christian ceremony in Hawai'i, a funeral service for one of his crew members.

Shortly after Cook left Hawai'i, he was forced to return due to a broken ship mast. By then the *makahiki* festivities had ended and the natives' attitude toward Cook and his crew had changed. If they were truly divine, why would they have to return to land just because of a broken mast? This is what a mere mortal would do, not a god. Not to mention that

one of the crew members had died a few days earlier. Surely a *god* cannot die!

Cook had tried to take the local chief hostage in return for a small rowboat that a few natives had stolen from his ship. Needless to say, Cook was killed here shortly after returning to land, and a memorial can be seen across the Bay.

To access the memorial, you need to park at the very top of Napo'opo Rd near the trailhead. The hike takes about an hour, and the terrain is rather rocky, so best hike with good shoes.

**First I'll plant the land
with wheatgrass to feed the earth
Their growth will paint the plot with
vibrant green
And echo the form of the yin-yang stone
down from the pebble pile
above the birthing compost soil
inside Kealakekua's coil
where the land whirls toward
the vortex bay**

Waimea Vortex

Vortex Type: Healing
Strength: Moderate
Public Access: Yes
Fee: No
Attractions: Labyrinth

Quick Fact: This location has been known for centuries as *Makahikilu,* a well known meeting place of the ancient Hawaiians.

How to Get There:
From Kona, take Palani Rd all the way to Waimea. From Hilo, take Hwy 19 north all the way to Waimea. Follow signs to hospital.

The North Hawai'i Community Hospital is the location of our next vortex. Located in the town of Waimea and serving 30,000 residents, the hospital has developed an international reputation as a center of healing that blends Eastern and Western healing approaches. The hospital features a prominent labyrinth right out front that was built to encourage patients as well as visitors to share in the healing. Labyrinths are temples that enhance and balance and bring a sense of the sacred - a place where we

can confirm our unity with the cosmos, awaken our vital force and elevate our consciousness. These structures are space/time temples where we can behold realities that oddly enough transcend space and time. The orientation, form and geometry of a labyrinth have symbolic as well as spatial importance. It is a mirror for the divine, a place to behold the beauty in nature.

Check out http://youtu.be/0UuhcamRz3s for a quick video.

Spiraling inward and out, this serpentine flow is the most generative form of subtle energy. The process of moving through the pathway unwinds this

stored energy, releasing, magnifying, and ultimately harnessing the flow. Working directly in conjunction with the human energy fields this spiraling flow interacts with the kundalini energy coiled at the base of our spine converting the subtle energy into life force itself. This uncoiling of the kundalini vitalizes us through a process of unfolding both upwards and inwards, an exhalation and ingathering of energies known as the dance of creation.

Why it's Sacred:

Labyrinths are known as sacred gateways and have been found at the entrance of ancient sites around the world. Often located at the center of subtle 'earth energies' these temples enhance, balance, regenerate and confirm our unity with the cosmos. A type of Labyrinth known as a Yantra was used as a meditation by Hindu midwives to assist in childbirth and served as a means of relaxation for the birth canal, another labyrinthine form.

The spiral is the most generative form of subtle energy. When its coil is unwound the stored energy is released. The areas where straight ley lines cross, or where underground water run are places to build sacred temples, labyrinths. These places are rich in both yin and yang (yin underground water crossing yang energy lines). The labyrinth resonates to this numinous spiral, the Phi ratio known as the 'Golden Mean' found in all of nature.

According to the book "The Art of Business: In The Footsteps of Giants", former CEO of the hospital Patrick Linton is said to have claimed that the hospital was situated in the center of an energy vortex formed by the five majestic volcanoes: Mauna Kea, Mauna Loa, Hualalai, Kohala, and Haleakala.

Native Hawaiians have many sacred myths about this energy vortex, believing that it links them with the heavens.

Waipio Valley Vortex

Vortex Type: Healing
Strength: Moderate
Public Access: Yes
Fee: No
Attractions: Black sand beach, Z trail, freshwater springs, swimming, boarding, hiking

Quick Fact: Waipio valley was the site of the final scene in the 1995 sci-fi film *Waterworld*, at which the main characters found dry land.

How to Get There:
Distance from Kona: 62.8 miles north | Distance from Hilo: 50.3 miles north

The best way to access our next vortex destination for the first time would be to try and take the local 4WD shuttle that provides rides up and down the mountain. There is a nice lookout at the top entrance to this valley, and this is where you can most likely find a ride. Some folks prefer the steep hike down into the valley, while others prefer taking their own trucks for some good old fashioned 4x4ing.

Once you have descended the mountain, otherwise known as the road into Waipio, you can choose to go further back into the valley, where some of the best hiking on the island is now at your feet, or you can turn back towards the beach and try to make it there without getting too wet. From what I recall, there are enormous mud pits that must be crossed to access the beach, but it's entirely worth it. I've also heard of a trail that leads to the beach, but could never find it.

Aerial photograph of Waipio Valley, home to many ancient kings

Why it's Sacred:

Waipio Valley is a sacred destination for many reasons. Ancient Hawaiian kings chose to call this place home. Underground springs give water and subsequently give life here. "Waipio" means "curved water" in the Hawaiian language, a possible reference to the vortex in the area.

The valley was the capital and residence of many early Hawaiian aliʻi (kings) up until the time of King ʻUmi. A place celebrated for its nioi tree (*Eugenia reinwardtiana*) known as the "Nioi wela o Paʻakalana" (The burning Nioi of Paʻakalana). It was the location of a grass palace belonging to the ancient kings of Hawaiʻi with the nioi stands. Kahekili II raided Waipiʻo in the 18th century and burned the four sacred trees to the ground and the palace no longer remains.

A magnificent black sand beach stretches for what seems like miles down the coast. Surfers and

boogie-boarders will love it here, and are often spotted at the dawn hours hoping to catch the first good wave of the day. The swell can get quite big, so be careful. Sunrises here are among the best in the world.

The valley floor at sea level is nearly 2,000 ft below the surrounding terrain, as you probably noticed on your way down the steep road. If classified as an official road, it would be the steepest road of its length in the United States and possibly the world. A few private taro farms are located in the valley. Several large waterfalls fall feed the river which flows from the foot of the largest falls at the back of the valley out to the ocean.

Hamakulia Vortex

Vortex Type: Vile

Coordinates: 26.57N | 148.8W

Quick Fact: The Hamakulia vortex is one of twelve vile vortices across the planet, similar to the Bermuda Triangle and Japan's Devil's Sea.

The next vortice I will be covering in this guide is the one supposedly off the northeastern coast of the Big Island, approximately 600 miles offshore. Be it that we are dealing with a location out in the open ocean, it somewhat limits our access and the opportunity to visit in person.

You could say that the Hamakulia vortex is Hawai'i's own version of the "Bermuda Triangle". It lies on the same line of latitude that the Bermuda Triangle and other infamous triangles perfectly, as if following a geometric pattern (it is). When pyramids, volcanoes and vortexes align all across the planet, it deserves a second & honest look in my opinion. This fuels my passion for pyramids and ancient mysteries.

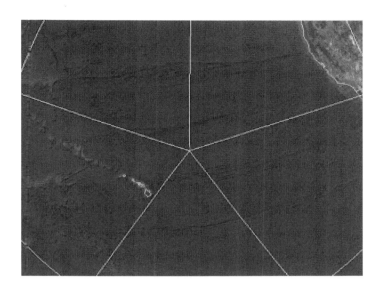

Biologist Ivan Sanderson theorized about 12 "vile vortices", one of them appearing just northeast of Hawai'i, known as Hamakulia.

With Hamakulia, being that we are dealing with a location in the open ocean it somewhat limits the number of phenomenon we can look for. Now, this isn't to say that this location is devoid of phenomena, it unfortunately means it may be going on without any witnesses. However, with all the shipping that goes on between Hawai'i and the mainland, don't you think someone would have noticed by now if ships and planes were missing?

As you can see with the image below there are moderate shipping interests that navigate this part of the ocean. The image shows just a one month window of traffic that flows through this part of the seas. If ships were disappearing, someone would probably have heard about it by now.

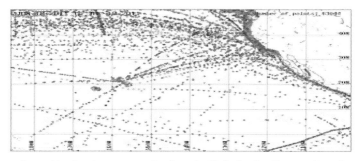

A graphic showing one month of sea traffic in the Pacific near Hawaii

Further exploration of the Hamakulia vortex using Google Earth has yielded no results. Nothing conclusive can be said about this vortex and the mystery goes on...but that doesn't mean it's not real.

Being that Hawai'i is located at the interface between two plates, it has been identified as being over a "hot spot"; however recent research is painting the Hawaiian hotspot in a new light. Please check out these two websites when you can.

http://newsoffice.mit.edu/2011/hawaii-hotspot-0527
http://www.mantleplumes.org/HawaiiBend.html

Wikipedia.com (*a website which can be altered and edited by anyone mind you*) defines a volcanic "hot spot" as:

*"The places known as **hot spots** or **hotspots** in geology are volcanic regions thought to be fed by underlying mantle that is anomalously hot compared with the mantle elsewhere. They may be on, near to, or far from tectonic plate boundaries. There are two hypotheses to explain them. One suggests that they are due to hot mantle plumes that rise as thermal diapirs from the core-mantle boundary. The other hypothesis postulates that it is not high temperature that causes the volcanism, but lithospheric extension that permits the passive rising of melt from shallow depths. This hypothesis considers the term "hotspot" to be a misnomer, asserting that the mantle source beneath them is, in fact, not anomalously hot at all."*

Now if we are to entertain the theory that the vile Vortexes are locations where anomalous phenomena occur than we must consider the

possibility that this location was more susceptible to becoming a "hot spot" due to the nearby vortex.

Either we are being misled by some of the tectonic / age data or we do not understand how the Hawaiian-Emperor chain formed.

Physicists are constantly shedding new light on the mysterious earth energy called gravity. New findings indicate Hawai'i may have been formed due to the help of gravity from the Great Pyramid of Giza. Due to the effect of *gravitational lensing*, a condensed beam of gravity is being directed through the Great Pyramid, through the earth, to Hawai'i and it could be ultimate reason behind the Hamakulia Vortex.

Author John Shaughnessy, who wrote the book "Pyramid Gravity Force", outlines why the larger pyramids were created, and that is to control the cooling and warming of planet Earth, much like a gigantic thermostat. He also created an entirely new law of gravity called Hexagontum Physics to back up his work.

According to the book, ancient *geo-engineers* built the main pyramids in order to control volcanic eruptions, and thus the warming/cooling of the planet. There are three major pyramid/volcano systems which control the earth's temperature, two of which are no longer functioning as they were created to do.

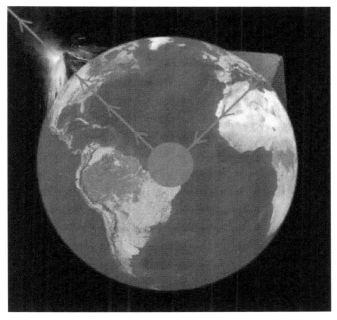

IMAGE: The Great Pyramid is 180 degrees away from Hawai'i, on the same line of latitude. Gravity is condensed and directed to the Earth's core, and out at a 90 degree angle, to Hawai'i. Is this the source of the Hawaiian "Hot Spot"?

The only remaining system in effect today is the *Giza Pyramid / Hawaiian Hotspot* system, which Hawai'i is where we currently and home to one of the most active volcanoes on Earth, so I felt the need to include all this.

Hawaii's connection to the Great Pyramid and essentially the "World Grid" is painfully obvious, and we're beginning to get a glimpse of the bigger picture now. At this moment everyone in Hawai'i is directly experiencing the gravity force coming from the Giza pyramid through the center of the earth to the Hawaiian hotspot....how's that for some awesome!!

Here's how John puts it:
"Pyramid Gravity Force will prove beyond a shadow of a doubt that mans past and present destructive penetration into planet Earths pyramid's has been the cause of many natural disasters around the world; The pyramids were built to prevent and/or control tectonic plate movement, volcanic activity, tidal waves, major earth quakes, land movements and the magnetic field movements here on Earth.

"The ancient pyramid architects refer to gravity as the divine energy source not electricity as some scholars would have you believe. The Egyptian hieroglyphs depict the snake as divine energy gravity, the Sun disc is colored red and the snake's body encompasses the sun disc, the energy that powers the sun is gravity.

"The Great Pyramid of Giza has one major energy output and that is a condensed gravity beam that shoots straight out the bottom of the pyramid to the center of the Earth's solid iron core, this graviton beam then ricochets out to the exact opposite side of the planet approximately 180 degrees from said pyramid and roughly at the same latitude. This gravity beam lowers the gravitational fields roughly at the same latitude on the exact opposite side of the Earth or 180 degrees from the pyramid.

"If you look at the Hawaiian Island chain, they are virtually a mirror image of the three large pyramids on the Nile River. Egypt's pyramids lowered the gravitational fields, which makes magma lighter, and it rises up from under miles of ocean water. Both the

Nile Valley pyramids and the Hawaiian Islands are on the same latitude.

Geological samples drilled from the depths of the Big Island dated back only 28,000 years, which is weird considering the age of the other volcanic islands around the globe. Some say the Hawaiian Islands are over one million years old, but core samples have not been found to verify that claim.

This Hawaiian mountain/island mass would have an equalization effect on the gravity beam being shot out of the pyramids in Egypt. When gravity readings were taken over both land masses, they closely matched, and they still do today. Both geographical locations have identical gravity fields over them. But keep in mind the Great Pyramid of Giza has been crippled due to human intervention."

John Shaughnessy, <u>Pyramid Gravity Force</u>

We have just learned that Hawai'i and the pyramids at Giza are connected, if not by gravity, then by latitude. But what if John's theory about the

formation of Hawai'i is indeed correct and certain gravitational anomalies were responsible for creating this isolated archipelago?

In my first book, *Pyramid Rising: Planetary Acupuncture to Combat Climate Change*, I wrote something very similar to what John has just told us. I wrote how larger and more frequent earthquakes were taking place around the world today and they were somehow connected to the World Grid, and that pyramids were the key to minimizing them and stopping further cataclysmic natural disasters from happening:

"The ancient wisdom tells us that human beings and the Earth are constructed similarly. The human being has a physical body and so does the Earth.

"A person has 7 energy bodies and a system of energy channels and the Earth has the same arrangement. It also has acupuncture points on its surface – the "places of power" that are associated with geological faults (channels carrying energy). But in the case of the Earth, the "needles" that should be

used are pyramids, the energy flow from which penetrates deep into the Earth's energy system and is capable of influencing its structure, alleviating tension and local excess build-ups.

"This idea was one of the main reasons established in deep antiquity that led to the creation of pyramid complexes in a belt around the Earth from East to West. Many of those pyramids have not survived." (Read a preview of Pyramid Rising in the back of this book.)

I felt John and I were totally on the exact same wavelength, wouldn't you agree; simply using different words to tell our story. Needless to say, we are now good friends, keeping in touch when time allows. John and I are just two writers out of a handful of bold authors who believe the ancient pyramids play a major role in climate change. I saw the connection between quakes and pyramids taking place on a map I was making at the time, and then I came across Pyramid Gravity Force.

More so than not I was noticing quakes occurring very close to the alleged Grid spots and not only did I see the connection in front of me, I felt a deeper connection existed, one the Ancients builders knew about. What's even stranger is that we published our books just four days apart, cosmic synchronistic timing if you ask me. We were both definitely on the same pyramid gravity wave, and it continues to this day, with me being inspired to write this book and including this particular chapter. *But back to Hamakulia…how does it all tie in together?*

Up until now, no one has presented a clear and precise reason for the alleged Vortexes to occur. But we have just learned again that the Earth itself has energies that can't be explained and that an *artificial* pyramid gravity force is possibly affecting them. Maybe that's why they were built, the pyramids, because up until now, no one really knows. The debate is ongoing and getting nowhere it seems. It's not a tomb. That much is apparent, however many other alternative theories exist what the Great Pyramid was created for, from a water heater to an energy machine. This is neither the time nor the

place to debate what they were created for; it was my intention to highlight a specific theory about Hawai'i and the pyramid gravity force.

Speaking of pyramids, what if there were supposedly pyramids near where the Hamakulia vortex is said to be? Surfacing online in time for this book comes the following pictures, of what appears to be underwater pyramids at the exact spot of the Hamakulia vortex. You can't make this stuff up! Well, actually, you can, and I'm well aware of that.

What appears to be pyramids near Hamakulia emitting energy?

I'm not saying this photo is actually real; I'm just pointing out that it exists and that I know about it, and now so do you.

Fact or Faked? Supposed pyramids near the Hamakulia Vortex

There's also the report of the alleged pyramids in the Bermuda Triangle vile vortex that resurfaced in 2012, thanks in part to an article I wrote called *"Pyramids of Glass Submerged in the Bermuda Triangle"* on my website ApparentlyApparel.com, sparking a huge internet following into the matter. Researchers in the area found what appeared to be underwater pyramids off the coast of Cuba. Researcher Graham Hancock is

planning a visit to the area to investigate as a follow up to his book, "*Fingerprints of the Gods.*"

This topic of pyramids, vile vortices, and Hawaii's healing energy is growing as fast as the island is, people from all around the world are being called here, that's why we need to pull together the resources needed to investigate these vortexes using modern technology and resources. It would appear science has turned a blind eye towards these mysteries, leaving it for independent researchers to explore.

Travel Notes:

Other Famous Vortexes

There are many famous energy vortexes in the USA and around the world. These include *Mystery Spot*, California; *Mystery Spot*, Michigan; *Confusion Hill*, California; *Wonder Spot*, Wisconsin; *Oregon Vortex*, *House of Mystery*, Montana; *Spook Hill*, Florida; and *Mystery Hill*, North Carolina to name a few. Other modern vortex sites include Sedona, Arizona and Taos, New Mexico...but while writing this book author Martin Gray shared with me that Sedona, Arizona is mostly just new age hype and not a vortex at all, yet I have met people who swear it is. I'd love to get there and see/feel for myself!

There are also vortexes that nobody knows about yet (*hint hint, get exploring!)* The world is still a large and very mysterious place, despite modern conveniences like Google Earth and the Internet.

Some Vortexes are *vile* since they are said to present devastating effects on objects, which may account for missing airplanes and ships. Others are associated with spiritual awakenings, "acts of God",

miracles and even physical healings, hence the sacred classification.

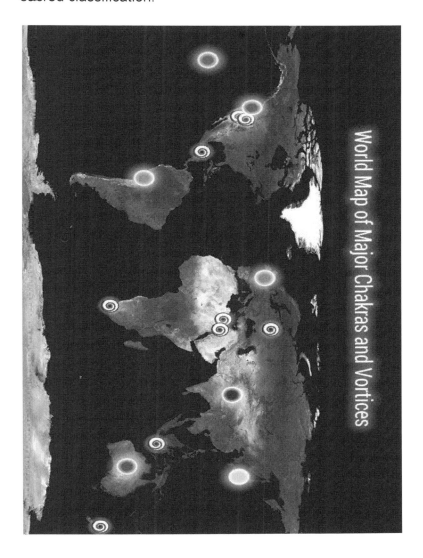

Besides the worldwide sites shown on the previous page, there are some quite powerful vortexes in the United States. Native cultures of the Americas knew about these sites, that much is evident due to the glyphs marking these sites. The most notable vortexes are probably the Oregon Vortex, Mount Shasta Vortex, and the four Sedona, Arizona vortexes. Superstition Mountain, Arizona is also the home of vortexes. However, unlike the previous three which are more or less permanent, easily sought out and experienced by crowds of tourists, lay persons, and New Agers, the vortexes in the Superstition Mountains, although equally as powerful or maybe even more so, are much more mysterious, subtle, and depend on the coming together of certain, but not always known to all. Also considered by some as vortex hot spots, and coincidentally, ALL in Arizona for some reason, are certain areas of the Grand Canyon, Sunset Crater, and the 50,000 year old meteorite impact site known as Meteor Crater.

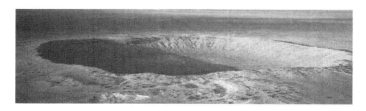

A New Beginning

When viewed from a distance it is sometimes difficult to separate real vortexes from the fake ones. There are spots today that are tourist attractions and some that have never been developed. Some Internet lists of these places include a place called the Tully House, which is just a part of a larger tourist stop called Clark's Trading Post, which includes other attractions in central New Hampshire. The odd thing here is that the owner doesn't claim a vortex, and indeed up the road from the nearby town of Lincoln there is evidence of an active vortex. So, the lore somehow knows there is a vortex in the area, but really doesn't know where it is. If the eastern Bermuda Triangle line from Puerto Rico up to Bermuda is continued straight northwest, the line will end or intersect at or near North Woodstock, New Hampshire.

The Internet is rife with mention of these spots in many different countries, especially the stretch of road variety, but I have chosen not to list them because I can't yet verify any of them. If readers know of others that are real, I will include it in

the next edition of this guide. I'd be delighted to see and share any unusual photographs that you send me.

I offer Hawaii Island vortex tours to the sites mentioned in this book all year round, as well as consulting services about existing vortexes and people that wish to upgrade their demonstrations, or to anyone wishing to start a new vortex attraction. These are strange businesses as well as strange areas and oddly they tend to promote each other. When people first visit a vortex, the first question usually is, "Are there any others?" After seeing one place people want to see more of them.

I hope this book has helped further knowledge of these peculiar earth anomalies called vortexes, and that this guide has convinced some that reality can at times be just a little different than what we have grown up experiencing. I also hope it has encouraged repeat visits, if not to the vortex originally visited, then to others along the way.

Returning Home

Thanks again for joining me on this one-of-a-kind adventure here on the Big Island. I hope my experiences have opened up new avenues of exploration for you. Learning from you is a vital part of my vortex research so I welcome you to be in touch with me with your experiences of these vortexes.

Send your letters, stories and photos of your adventure to:

Hawai'i Vortex Field Guide

P.O. Box 659

Captain Cook, HI 96704

Email: director@kahunaresearchgroup.org

Website: http://www.ZachRoyer.com

Please feel free to leave a review or comment of this book (and of your hike) at Amazon.com or ZachRoyer.com. That would really help out, thanks!

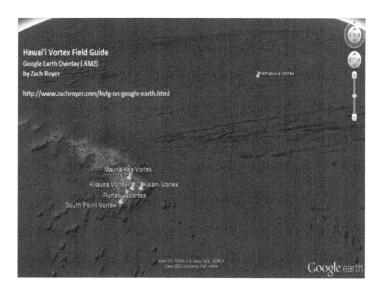

BONUS:

Hawai'i Vortex Field Guide on Google Earth
(Downloadable .KMZ file)

As an added value, you can download the Google Earth overlay that goes with this book at:

http://www.zachroyer.com/hvfg-on-google-earth.html

The web page above is not visible on my website; it's only listed in this book for readers and supporters. Once downloaded and installed, you're just click one click away from any vortex in this book. Click to zoom in and see what's there; you will be amazed, as was I. Aloha!

About the Author

Zach Royer is an independent researcher, author, world explorer as well as the director of Hawaii's premier anomalous research organization, Kahuna Research Group, where he has spent the last five years at the forefront of exploring Hawaii's secrets & mysteries. His work has been featured on the Travel Channel, in the Journal of Anomalous Sciences, as well as in numerous travel magazines and on many different websites over the last few years.

Zach was born and raised in Washington State, attended college in Colorado for environmental science and now lives in Hawaii most of the year. Once upon a time, he worked as a landscape & maintenance technician, a designer in the apparel industry and a manager at a hobby store, but has been researching and writing full time for several years. (He doesn't miss retail. At all.) Most of all, he's thankful that he gets to make a living doing what he loves and considers himself pretty much the luckiest guy on the planet.

Zach currently leads sacred vortex tours and historical ghost tours on Hawai'i Island, the most historic and supernatural of all the Hawaiian Islands, and he welcomes you to join him. Visit his blog http://ZachRoyer.com to see what adventure he is planning next...

A quick message from the author:

I really love helping people. It is a passion of mine. I'd love to be able to help you publish your manuscript into your next book, so I am offering professional author services as of November 1, 2014 to anyone in need.

Becoming a published author changed my life in ways I never imagined. You meet incredible people along the way who become friends for life, as well as fellow authors, magazine editors, TV producers, news crews and much more. I welcome you to contact me today, and let me do my best to help you become a published author.

After publishing a few books on my own, I've become quite familiar with the process of writing, editing, formatting, cover design, the entire Amazon/CreateSpace process, book royalties collection, and so now I help others. Let me share my years of experience with you by working on your next book project.   *Aloha, Z.R.*

References for HVFG

"Scientific Vortex Information" by Pete A. Sanders, Jr

"Vortex Field Guide" by Vortex Research Group

"The Secrets & Mysteries of Hawaii" by Pila Chiles

"Earth Energies" by Serge Kahili King

"Sedona Vortex 2000" by Richard Dannelley

"Pyramid Gravity Force" by John Shaughnessy

Websites

http://SaredSites.com

http://Paleaku.com

http://Kalani.com

http://KahunaResearchGroup.org/equipment

http://VortexHunters.com

http://VortexMaps.com

http://Wikipedia.com

http://ZachRoyer.com/hvfg-on-google-earth.html

http://Spiritofmaat.com/archive/nov2/vortex.htm

http://www.HawaiiLife.com/articles/2012/10/hawaii-healing/

New Hotspot Theories

http://newsoffice.mit.edu/2011/hawaii-hotspot-0527
http://Mantleplumes.org/HawaiiBend.html

THIS IS A PREVIEW OF
Pyramid Rising
By Zach Royer

Introduction

By plotting many large earthquakes that took place on or very near specific 'World Grid' sites, such as Giza, Stonehenge, Tiahuanaco, and at many other Grid locations, I have noticed a definite correlation between these megalithic sites and heightened seismic activity. A relationship between the cyclical earth changes, natural disasters and these magnificent structures has become apparent. Modern day researchers are beginning to explore in detail these mysteries, investigating what is referred to as the "Planetary Grid" or the Earth's energy meridian system – a system as old as the earth itself.

Two ideas came to mind when wondering why someone would go out of their way to place giant pyramids all throughout the world, on certain "hot-spots" of seismic energy and fault lines. My overall conclusions were startling to say the least!

Idea One - Pyramids and megaliths (rock structures) were erected at these specific energetic sites and along certain lines in the landscape to help

with stabilizing the earth's overall seismic energy. [After the destruction of Lemuria/Mu and Atlantis, the surviving civilizations were seemingly obsessed with building earthquake-proof structures (evidence is all over the planet) and eventually figured out how to combine all of their sciences into one structure - the Pyramid.

Idea Two - Pyramids and megaliths were placed by these high energy locations to form a "grid" much like today's power grid, to "tap" in to a planetary energy source capable of producing useable electricity and distributing it across the globe in an amazing fashion, something Tesla almost did using Wardenclyffe.... (Google *Tesla and the Great Pyramid of Giza*)

What exactly did our ancestors try to tell us, by placing these structures where they did? Does it have to do with geo-engineering or climate change?

Chapter 1

Reviving the Past – Surviving the Future

The planetary clock has since moved past the winter solstice of 2012, yet prophecies about "the End of the World" and the inevitable destruction of the greater part of the human race is still discussed on our TV screens, internet chat rooms, and in general throughout all of our media outlets. In the scenarios most often suggested the Earth's future is presented as a succession of planetary-scale catastrophes, in the face of which a considerable portion of humanity helplessly awaits "the End." But the "End of the World" is not coming and the vast majority of the Earth's population will not perish, although serious trials and tribulations do lie ahead for humanity.

Coming events will unfold in close connection with processes taking place on the sun which began last year in late December, when solar activity reached its peak during the current solar cycle. Between the sixteenth and twenty-eighth of December 2012 (the phase of the winter solstice) the

planet's core began to radiate a flow of energy that, combined with the incoming solar radiation, stimulated the activity of processes in the Earth's bio- and geo-spheres. This has been observed by celestial observers for centuries, and it makes sense that if these forces were to prove deadly, something might have been done to prevent it. Super-powerful coronal discharges are bringing our planet magnetic storms of unprecedented force that are causing climatic and shorter-term weather anomalies, floods, earthquakes, tsunamis, fires, diseases and local conflict.

Don't believe me? Just watch the evening news. Chances are you or someone you know has had to deal with some type of weather related phenomenon lately, if not, consider yourself extremely lucky. I'm not exempt, either. Because I choose to live on a volcanic island in the middle of the Pacific Ocean, I have to worry about occasional hurricanes, tsunamis, earthquakes, lava flows, extreme isolation and more. But compared to what may hit other areas of the world, like extended drought for instance, I'll take my chances.

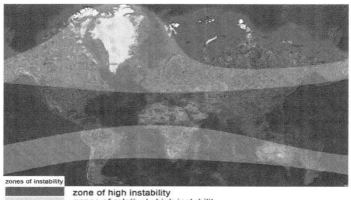

zones of instability
zone of high instability
zones of relatively high instability

According to scientists, there are zones of high instability on the Earth's surface that will last several decades from now. More areas will be affected by natural disasters than others. Although the coming events are going to be tough for humanity the future of civilization is not as hopeless as the ancient prophecies foretell. The Earth's human population is capable of influencing the future in a practical way, moderating the gravity of coming events and moving from passive expectation to positive action.

The technology for exerting such an influence on Earth was known and used effectively in the very remote past. It is interesting and useful to us,

because it is capable of reducing the impact and consequences of the approaching cataclysms. To employ this lost and forgotten geo-engineering pyramid technology we will need to undertake a series of practical steps to create a means (tool) of influence. To understand the mechanism by which future events might be influenced, let us begin with the premise that unprecedentedly powerful solar and magnetic storms will cause a sharp surge in the intensity of the Earth's magnetic field and increased tension in the planet's energy system (the conductivity of its energy channels).

The Earth is a living cosmic organism that reacts with great sensitivity to external factors. At the end of the first decade of the new millennium that organism is profoundly "ill" due to humanity's immoral industrial and economic activities. When the Earth, as an organism, initiates the self-healing and self-cleansing processes, the planet is subject to earthquakes and anomalous weather conditions. These conditions are key components that function within the Earth's immune system which are then compounded by a multitude of influences from outer space. Now let us turn our attention to the wisdom of

the ancients by drawing certain parallels to ourselves, and in doing so, emphasize distinct correlations that will help us to understand the logic of the ancients and provide a way to solve our problem.

When human beings fall seriously ill, their body temperature rises and their general condition worsens. The organism is in a state of stress and thus zones of excess energy appear in the energy system. Any external influence causes unhealthy reactions, like the shaking of the body, pains and even convulsions... When exposed to negative factors (such as solar and magnetic storms), the heightened tension in the Earth's magnetic field causes corresponding immune reactions: a worsening of the physical condition and even agony as we see in our bodies.

In such cases people in the East have traditionally resorted to a method of combating the illness by inserting needles into specific acupuncture points on the human body. These needles act something like lightning conductors, discharging the excess energy in a particular area, and after which

the illness goes into recession and the organism calms down.

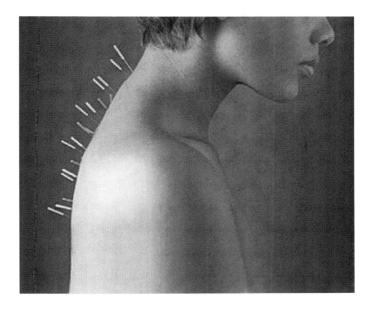

The ancient wisdom tells us that human beings and the Earth are constructed similarly, with the human being and the earth both having seven energy bodies within their physical bodies. Since humans have acupuncture points, so too does the earth, which are entitled as, "places of power."

These places of power are associated with geological faults (channels that carry energy). In the case of the Earth, these 'needles' (the areas used for acupuncture) are the pyramids, as these structures allow for energy to flow from the core of the Earth by penetrating deep into the Earth's energy system. These needles are capable of influencing the structure, and alleviating tension and local excess buildups.

END OF PREVIEW

Thanks for Reading!

Order a copy at ZachRoyer.com

Or Amazon.com today.

Pyramid Rising:

Planetary Acupuncture to Combat Climate Change

Based on years of study into environmental science, climate change, natural disasters, worldwide famine and planetary unbalance -- coupled with my life-long thirst of ancient history (and mystery), I truly believe that most of the unusual ancient structures like Stonehenge and the pyramids of Giza were built to interact with the Earth's energies, forces of nature such as magnetism, gravity, light, heat, and telluric energy, possibly providing electricity to ancient mankind. Human beings seek acupuncture for certain ailments, when energy pathways, known as meridians, are blocked, a condition which can lead to disease and fatigue. The human body and the earth are constructed in a similar way, the saying "As Above, So Below" is more than just a saying...it's a universal Truth. I emphasize that in this book. Think of it as acupuncture on a planetary scale...

Paperback: 140 pages, black & white photos | 8" x 5" size
Place your order or learn more at
http://ZachRoyer.com.